I0764162

Metaphysics

Aristotle's Ultimate Exploration of Reality, Existence, and Knowledge

A Modern Translation

Adapted for the Contemporary Reader

Aristotle

Table of Contents

Preface - Message to the Reader

Rebuilding the Greatest Library in Human History

Thousands of years ago, the Library of Alexandria was the heart of global knowledge — a sanctuary where the wisdom of every known civilization was gathered and shared freely.

And then, it was lost.

Now, we're rebuilding it — and you are invited to join us.

At the Library of Alexandria, we've set out to make every book available to *every person on Earth* — not just in print, but in every language, every format, and for every reader.

Here's how we do it:

- **Deluxe Print Editions at True Printing Cost** - Order any book as a high-quality paperback, elegant hardcover, or stunning boxset — and only pay what it costs to print. No markups. No middlemen.
- **Unlimited Access to the Greatest Works** - Enjoy thousands of timeless classics — from Plato to Shakespeare to Tolstoy — in beautiful, modern eBook and audiobook editions. Read and listen without limits — for every reader, everywhere.
- **Modern Translations for Every Language & Dialect** - We're reimagining the classics in clear, accessible language — and translating them into every dialect imaginable. Everyone deserves to understand humanity's greatest ideas.

When you visit **LibraryofAlexandria.com**, you're not just accessing books — you're joining a global movement to restore, preserve, and share the wisdom of civilization.

Join us today at LibraryofAlexandria.com

Together, we'll ensure the light of human wisdom never fades again.

With gratitude,
The Modern Library of Alexandria Team

Visit:

www.libraryofalexandria.com

Or scan the code below:

Introduction

Ancient Greece was a civilization famous for its great contributions to philosophy, politics, art, and science. It thrived from the 8th century BCE until the Roman Empire started to decline. Greece's city-states, especially Athens, were the heart of culture and intellectual thought. This was the time when democracy began, impressive buildings like the Parthenon were built, and famous playwrights like Sophocles and Euripides produced their works. The Greeks' curiosity about the world around them laid the foundation for Western philosophy. Thinkers like Socrates, Plato, and later Aristotle, pushed the limits of what people understood about the world.

Greek society was deeply connected to theism, which focused on a large group of gods and goddesses who were believed to control every part of life. But this system did not prevent people from exploring new ideas. In fact, it coexisted with a growing interest in finding logical explanations for nature and human life. Intellectuals would often debate and discuss these ideas in public places like the Agora. Aristotle grew up in this dynamic environment, learning from earlier philosophers, and later challenging and expanding their ideas.

Aristotle's Life

Aristotle was born in 384 BCE in a small town called Stagira, located in northern Greece. His father, Nicomachus, was a doctor for King Amyntas of Macedon, and this allowed Aristotle to be around the Macedonian royal court from a young age. When his parents passed away, Aristotle was sent to Athens at the age of 17 to pursue his education. Athens was the center of intellectual life in Greece, and Aristotle joined Plato's Academy, which was the most respected school of the time. The Academy was a place where students discussed everything from ethics to science. Although Aristotle learned a lot from Plato, he did not always agree with him, especially when it came to metaphysics, which deals with the nature of reality.

After spending almost 20 years at the Academy, Aristotle left Athens around 347 BCE after Plato's death. He traveled around different cities in Greece, continuing to study and learn. In 343 BCE, he was invited to the court of King Philip II of Macedon, where he became the tutor of Philip's son, Alexander, who would later become known as Alexander the Great. Aristotle taught Alexander about philosophy, ethics, politics, and science. Aristotle's influence is visible in Alexander's leadership style, which showed respect for knowledge and strategic thinking.

After teaching Alexander, Aristotle returned to Athens in 335 BCE, where he opened his own school called the Lyceum. Unlike Plato's Academy, the Lyceum focused more on recording knowledge and observing nature. Aristotle and his students performed research, studied animals, and took notes on what they observed. The Lyceum became a major center of learning, and it rivaled Plato's Academy. This is also where Aristotle wrote many of his famous works.

Later in life, after the death of Alexander in 323 BCE, the political climate in Athens became difficult for Aristotle because of his connections to the Macedonian court. Accused of disrespecting the gods, Aristotle decided to leave Athens. He fled to Chalcis, where he passed away in 322 BCE. Even though he had to leave Athens, his legacy lived on through his many writings and the influence of his school, the Lyceum.

Aristotle's Impact on Western Thought

No figure looms larger over the development of Western philosophy and science than Aristotle. A student of Plato and tutor to Alexander the Great, he unified logic, ethics, politics, rhetoric, and metaphysics into a coherent system that shaped intellectual inquiry for centuries. Although his writings reflect the best knowledge of his era, they also reveal a distinctive way of understanding the world—one that balances observation with rigorous logical analysis. Over time, this method has profoundly influenced everything from political theory to modern scientific methodology.

Aristotle approached knowledge as an interconnected whole, seeing each field of study as a vital path toward truth. While many earlier thinkers focused on abstract concepts, he emphasized direct observation of the natural world. By systematically examining and classifying what he saw, Aristotle laid the groundwork for the empirical methods now central to modern science. Although our understanding of nature has evolved, his legacy endures in today's emphasis on evidence-based research.

Logic: The Foundation of Rational Inquiry

Often hailed as the "father of formal logic," Aristotle introduced a system of reasoning that shaped intellectual discourse for over two millennia. In works like the Organon, he analyzed how valid conclusions are drawn from premises and introduced syllogisms—deductive arguments that became standard tools in philosophy, theology, and science. Even contemporary logic, despite its modern mathematical and symbolic advancements, can trace many of its core principles back to Aristotle's pioneering analyses.

Metaphysics: Exploring the Nature of Reality

Aristotle's Metaphysics offered one of the earliest comprehensive explorations of existence at its most fundamental level. There, he described the nature of "being qua being" and introduced the concepts of potentiality and actuality to explain how things change and develop. These ideas deeply influenced medieval scholastics—both Christian and Islamic—who integrated Aristotelian reasoning into their theological frameworks. Today, discussions about consciousness, identity, and free will still reference these Aristotelian notions.

Ethics and the Pursuit of the Good Life

In the Nicomachean Ethics, Aristotle proposed that the ultimate aim of human life is eudaimonia, often translated as "happiness" or "flourishing." He argued that we achieve this through virtue, developed by cultivating good habits guided by reason. His famous Doctrine of the Mean asserts that moral virtue resides between two extremes—for instance, courage lies between recklessness and cowardice. This focus on character formation has profoundly shaped the tradition known as "virtue ethics," influencing modern debates on moral education, personal development, and what it means to live well.

Politics: The Role of the Individual in the City-State

Aristotle's practical approach to ethics naturally extended into political theory. In Politics, he explored various forms of government—monarchy, aristocracy, oligarchy, democracy—and weighed their merits and pitfalls. For Aristotle, a well-ordered polis (city-state) exists not merely for survival or trade but to enable its citizens to live virtuous, fulfilling lives. His conviction that ethics and politics are intertwined remains influential, informing contemporary discussions on citizenship, governance, and justice.

Rhetoric: The Art of Persuasion

In his treatise Rhetoric, Aristotle examined how persuasion works, detailing how arguments must appeal to ethos (credibility), pathos (emotion), and logos (logic). This clear framework for effective communication continues to guide public speakers, legal advocates, and writers. From ancient courtroom orations to modern political campaigns, Aristotelian rhetoric underpins many of the strategies people use to sway audiences and shape public opinion.

Beyond these core subjects, Aristotle made significant contributions to biology, physics, psychology, and aesthetics. In the Poetics, for example, he investigated why humans respond so powerfully to tragic drama, pioneering the concept of catharsis—the emotional release that audiences feel through art. Throughout the medieval period, thinkers like Thomas Aquinas integrated Aristotle's theories into Christian theology, while Islamic philosophers such as Avicenna and Averroes preserved, interpreted, and expanded upon his works.

Across centuries of reinterpretation and debate, Aristotle remains a living voice in contemporary thought. His insistence on systematically gathering evidence and connecting it to logical principles laid the foundation for what we now recognize as the scientific method. His inquiries into human flourishing, civic responsibility, and the nature of argument continue to spark discussion and inspire new research. From personal ethics to societal organization, Aristotle's ideas help us frame enduring questions about how best to live, learn, and understand reality.

In sum, Aristotle stands as a foundational pillar of Western thought. He bridged abstract theorizing and practical inquiry, bequeathing a vision of knowledge that values both reason and experience. From ethics and politics to science and art, his ideas have been woven into countless intellectual traditions. Even today, as we grapple with questions of morality, governance, and truth, we walk in the footsteps of an ancient thinker whose breadth of insight and depth of analysis continue to guide our pursuit of wisdom.

Final Thoughts

By preserving Aristotle's legacy, we protect the intellectual depth and rigor that defined his way of understanding the world. His systematic way of asking questions, his classification of knowledge, and his ethical theories are still relevant today, providing a model for critical thinking across many subjects. This preservation is important not just for philosophy students but for anyone interested in the foundations of human thought and the development of ideas that shape the world we live in.

One of the difficulties in studying Aristotle's work is that his ideas and language are complex. Translating these works into our modern language is a key step in making his profound insights easier for more people to understand. By putting his ideas into today's language, more readers can engage with his thoughts, even if they don't have a background in classical studies. Making Aristotle's work accessible means adapting them to modern ways of thinking without losing their original depth. This helps bridge the gap between ancient and modern readers, making sure Aristotle's work stays relevant.

Metaphysics

When it comes to predicting the future through dreams, we shouldn't quickly dismiss it as nonsense, but we also shouldn't fully trust it. The fact that many people believe dreams have special meanings makes us think there could be something to it, as it's based on real experiences. It's not impossible that some dreams could predict future events, which seems reasonable. This might make us believe that all dreams have some sort of meaning. However, the lack of any clear reason for this kind of prediction also makes us doubt it. For one thing, it seems strange to think that God would send dreams to predict the future but only to ordinary people, not to the wisest or best people. And if we take God out of the picture, none of the other explanations seem very likely either. How can it make sense that someone could dream about something happening far away, like at the ends of the Earth? Understanding that seems to go beyond what people are capable of.

So, we must think of these dreams as either causing events, being signs of events, or simply being coincidences. They could be all of these things, or just one of them. By "cause," I mean like how the moon causes a solar eclipse, or how being tired can cause a fever. By "sign," I mean like how the start of an eclipse shows it's happening, or how a rough tongue can be a sign of a fever. And by "coincidence," I mean like someone taking a walk during a solar eclipse—the walk doesn't cause the eclipse, and the eclipse doesn't cause the walk. That's why coincidences don't follow specific rules.

So, should we say that some dreams are causes and others are signs, like signs of things happening in the body? Doctors even say that we should pay attention to our dreams, and this makes sense for people who aren't doctors, too. Movements inside the body during the day are usually too small to notice because they are overshadowed by more obvious movements that happen while we are awake. But when we sleep, smaller movements seem bigger. This is clear from what often happens during sleep. For example, dreamers may think they hear thunder and lightning when it's just a faint ringing in their ears. Or they may think they're tasting honey or something sweet when it's only a little bit of phlegm in their throat. They might dream of walking through fire and feeling intense heat when it's just a slight warmth in part of their body. When they wake up, they realize what was really happening.

Since the beginnings of everything are small, this is also true for illnesses or other conditions about to affect the body. It's clear that these early signs are easier to notice when we are asleep than when we are awake.

It's also possible that some of the images that come to us in sleep can actually cause the actions related to them. When we are about to do something while awake or have just done something, we often dream about those actions. This happens because the movements of our dreams are connected to the movements we had during the day. In the same way, movements we experience in sleep could be the starting points for actions we take during the day. Our thoughts during the day may be linked to the images we saw during the night. So, it's possible that some dreams could be both signs and causes of future events.

Most dreams that are said to predict the future are just coincidences, especially those about strange things or events far away, like a sea battle, where the dreamer has no control over what happens. It's normal for people to sometimes mention something and then have it happen. So, why shouldn't this happen in dreams too? In fact, it's probably more likely to happen while we sleep. Just like saying someone's name doesn't cause them to show up, dreaming about something doesn't cause it to happen either—it's just a coincidence. This explains why many dreams don't come true, because coincidences don't follow specific rules.

Since even some animals dream, it's clear that dreams aren't sent by God to reveal the future. Dreams come from nature, which has a divine design, but nature itself isn't divine. One reason we know dreams aren't from God is that people who have vivid dreams or seem to predict the future often aren't the wisest or best people. This suggests that God isn't sending them dreams, but that some people who are more excitable or distracted just happen to have dreams that seem to predict real events. It's like playing a game of chance—if you guess enough times, you'll eventually guess correctly.

It's not surprising that many dreams don't come true, just like many weather predictions or signs of illness don't always turn out to be correct. For example, we might expect rain or wind based on certain signs, but if something else happens that's stronger, the rain or wind might not happen. In the same way, many things that people plan to do, no matter how well-planned, can be stopped by other, more powerful forces. Just because something was about to happen doesn't mean it will happen exactly as we expect. Still, we have to accept that the early signs of events are real, even if the event doesn't always follow.

As for dreams that don't seem to have natural signs and seem strange because of their timing, place, or scale, or when the dreamer has no control over the event, we shouldn't think of them as prophetic unless they're just coincidences. A better explanation than the one given by Democritus, who talked about "images" and "emanations," is this: When something causes movement in water or air, that movement continues even after the thing that caused it is gone. In the same way, a movement and a resulting perception can reach the mind during sleep, even if the cause is no longer there. This could explain how dreams can seem to predict the future, especially at night when the air is calm, and movements aren't disturbed like they are during the day when the air is more active. People are also more sensitive to small movements during sleep, which might explain why dreams seem to predict the future.

This could also explain why it's regular people, not the wisest ones, who seem to have prophetic dreams. If God were sending these dreams, they would happen during the day and to wise people. But since they don't, it makes sense that ordinary people have these dreams. These people don't spend much time thinking, so their minds are empty and easily moved by whatever comes along.

For people with mental illnesses, their normal thoughts don't get in the way of outside movements, which is why they seem to sense things more clearly. Some people have vivid dreams about people they know well because they are more concerned about those people. Just like friends can recognize each other from far away, they can also sense things about each other more easily in dreams. Familiar movements are easier to recognize. People with a lot of dark bile, who are more emotional, often "shoot from a distance" and hit the target, because their thoughts move quickly through their minds, just like people repeating lines from memory.

The best person to interpret dreams is someone who can see connections and similarities. Anyone can interpret clear and vivid dreams. By "seeing connections," I mean that dream images are like reflections in water, as we've said before. If the water is disturbed, the reflection looks nothing like the original image. A skilled interpreter can quickly recognize the scattered and distorted pieces of the reflection and see that they represent a person, a horse, or something else. In the same way, a dream is often like a blurry image, because the internal movements of the body make the dream unclear.

We've now discussed what sleep and dreams are, the causes behind them, and how dreams might be linked to predicting the future.

• • •

The End

Thank you for Reading

You've Just Read a Piece of the Greatest Library Ever Rebuilt

Thank you for reading.

This book is one of thousands we're restoring, reimagining, and translating as part of the **Modern Library of Alexandria** — a global movement to preserve and share humanity's most important ideas.

What was once lost to fire and time is now rising again — not just as memory, but as living, breathing knowledge, freely accessible to all.

What You Can Do Next:

- **Keep Reading.**

  Discover more legendary works — in beautiful print, audiobook, or digital form — at LibraryofAlexandria.com.

- **Build Your Own Library.**

  Every title is available as a paperback, hardcover, or collectible boxset — at true printing cost. Craft a personal library worthy of display.

- **Spread the Light.**

  Share this book. Tell others about the movement. Help us translate every timeless work into every language, so no reader is ever left behind.

By finishing this book, you've already taken part in something extraordinary.

Join us at LibraryofAlexandria.com

Together, we're rebuilding the greatest library the world has ever known.

With appreciation,
The Modern Library of Alexandria Team

Visit:

www.libraryofalexandria.com

Or scan the code below:

www.ingramcontent.com/pod-product-compliance
Lightning Source LLC
LaVergne TN
LVHW041942100826
845152LV00003B/57

9781804213940